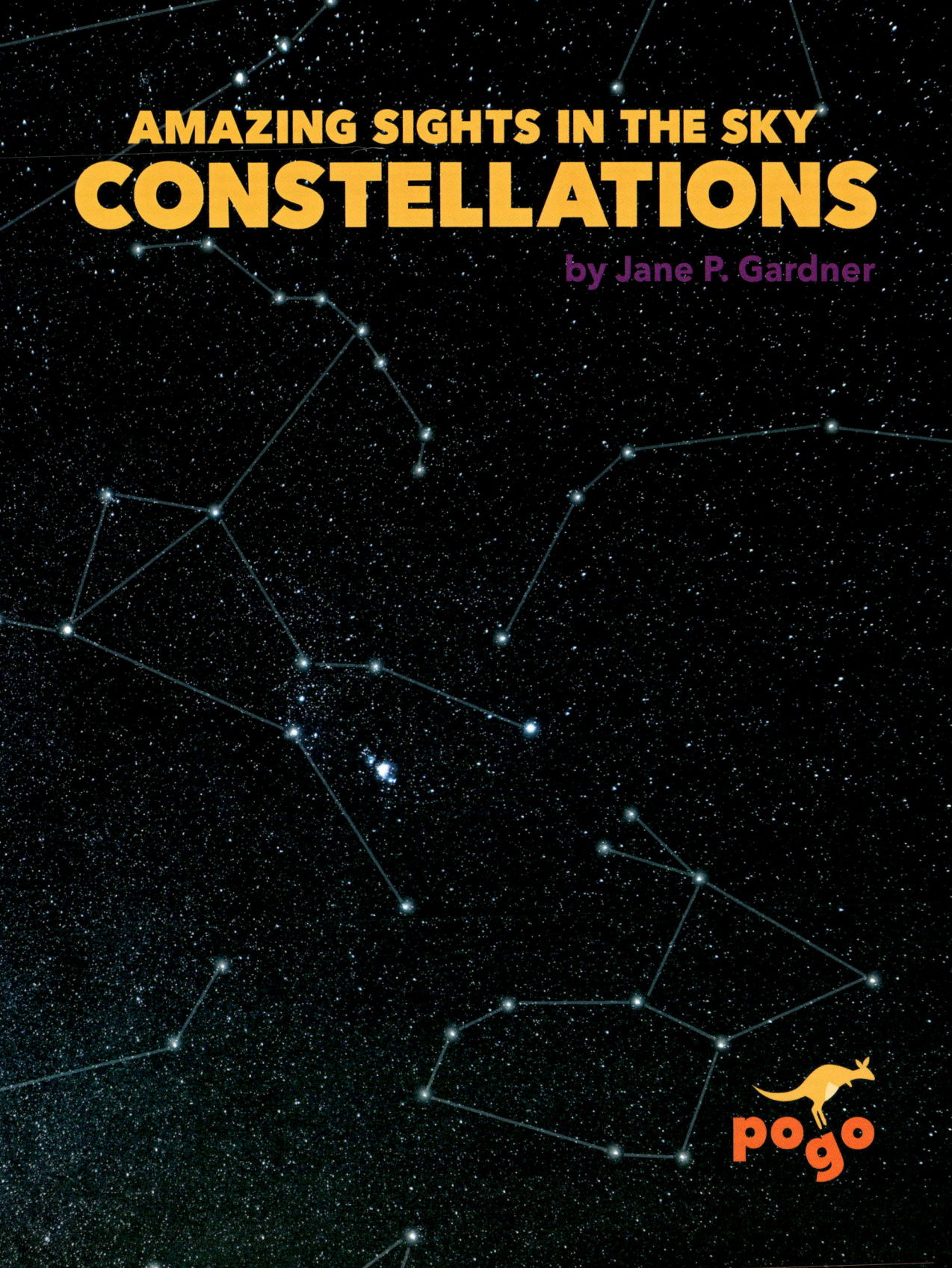

AMAZING SIGHTS IN THE SKY
CONSTELLATIONS

by Jane P. Gardner

pogo

Ideas for Parents and Teachers

Pogo Books let children practice reading informational text while introducing them to nonfiction features such as headings, labels, sidebars, maps, and diagrams, as well as a table of contents, glossary, and index.

Carefully leveled text with a strong photo match offers early fluent readers the support they need to succeed.

Before Reading

- "Walk" through the book and point out the various nonfiction features. Ask the student what purpose each feature serves.
- Look at the glossary together. Read and discuss the words.

Read the Book

- Have the child read the book independently.
- Invite him or her to list questions that arise from reading.

After Reading

- Discuss the child's questions. Talk about how he or she might find answers to those questions.
- Prompt the child to think more. Ask: What did you know about stars and constellations before you read this book? What more would you like to learn?

Pogo Books are published by Jump!
5357 Penn Avenue South
Minneapolis, MN 55419
www.jumplibrary.com

Copyright © 2021 Jump!
International copyright reserved in all countries.
No part of this book may be reproduced in any form without written permission from the publisher.

Library of Congress Cataloging-in-Publication Data

Names: Gardner, Jane P., author.
Title: Constellations / by Jane P. Gardner.
Description: Minneapolis, MN: Jump!, Inc., [2021]
Series: Amazing sights in the sky
Audience: Ages 7-10 | Audience: Grades 2-3
Identifiers: LCCN 2020008998 (print)
LCCN 2020008999 (ebook)
ISBN 9781645275596 (hardcover)
ISBN 9781645275602 (paperback)
ISBN 9781645275619 (ebook)
Subjects: LCSH: Constellations—Juvenile literature.
Stars—Juvenile literature.
Classification: LCC QB802 .G37 2021 (print)
LCC QB802 (ebook) | DDC 523.8—dc23
LC record available at https://lccn.loc.gov/2020008998
LC ebook record available at https://lccn.loc.gov/2020008999

Editor: Jenna Gleisner
Designer: Molly Ballanger

Photo Credits: Pike-28/Shutterstock, cover; shaunl/iStock, 1; trekandshoot/Shutterstock, 3; KIDSADA PHOTO/Shutterstock, 4; EyeEm/Alamy, 5; Alan Dyer/Stocktrek Images/Getty, 6-7; Pollyana Ventura/iStock, 8; SeryZone/Shutterstock, 9; Milosz_G/Shutterstock, 10-11; Erkki Makkonen/Shutterstock, 12-13; Brian Donovan/Shutterstock, 14-15; Allexxandar/Shutterstock, 16-17; Serrgey75/Shutterstock, 18-19; AN Photographer2463/Shutterstock, 20-21; THEPALMER/iStock, 23.

Printed in the United States of America at Corporate Graphics in North Mankato, Minnesota.

TABLE OF CONTENTS

CHAPTER 1
Patterns in the Sky..................................4

CHAPTER 2
The Science of Stars..............................8

CHAPTER 3
Discover the Patterns.........................14

ACTIVITIES & TOOLS
Try This!...22
Glossary..23
Index..24
To Learn More.....................................24

CHAPTER 1

PATTERNS IN THE SKY

On a dark night, you can look up and see a few thousand **stars**. There are many more out there!

Look closely. Some stars make patterns in the sky. We call these **constellations**. You might find a pattern shaped like a scorpion!

CHAPTER 1

People have observed these patterns for thousands of years. **Ancient** people named them. They even made up stories about them. Pegasus is said to be a horse.

Others were named by sailors or **astronomers**. Let's take a closer look at these patterns in the sky.

DID YOU KNOW?

How many constellations are there? There are 88 that have been officially recognized.

CHAPTER 1 — 7

CHAPTER 2

THE SCIENCE OF STARS

Constellations are stars. Look up in the sky. Do you see the sun? You are looking at a star! The sun is the closest star to Earth.

Sirius

Stars make their own heat and light. A star's **magnitude** describes how bright it appears to us on Earth. Sirius is the brightest star in our night sky.

CHAPTER 2 9

How a star looks depends on its size and distance from Earth. Closer stars look brighter. **Luminosity** describes a star's **energy**. Stars with more energy are brighter.

Look at any constellation. Let's use Gemini as an example. The stars seem to be close together. But they are actually very far apart. We see the pattern because of our **point of view**. If we were close to the stars, we wouldn't see the pattern. Do you see the twins holding hands?

CHAPTER 3
DISCOVER THE PATTERNS

Some constellations are visible on clear nights year-round.

Southern Cross

The Southern Cross is one. It is visible in the **Southern Hemisphere**. It always appears in the night sky.

Have you seen the Big Dipper? It can be easy to find on clear nights. It is an **asterism**. What does this mean? It is a pattern. But it is smaller than a constellation. The Big Dipper is actually part of Ursa Major! Ursa Major and Ursa Minor are always visible in the **Northern Hemisphere**.

DID YOU KNOW?

The Big Dipper has been used for **navigation**. Why? It points toward the North Star.

CHAPTER 3

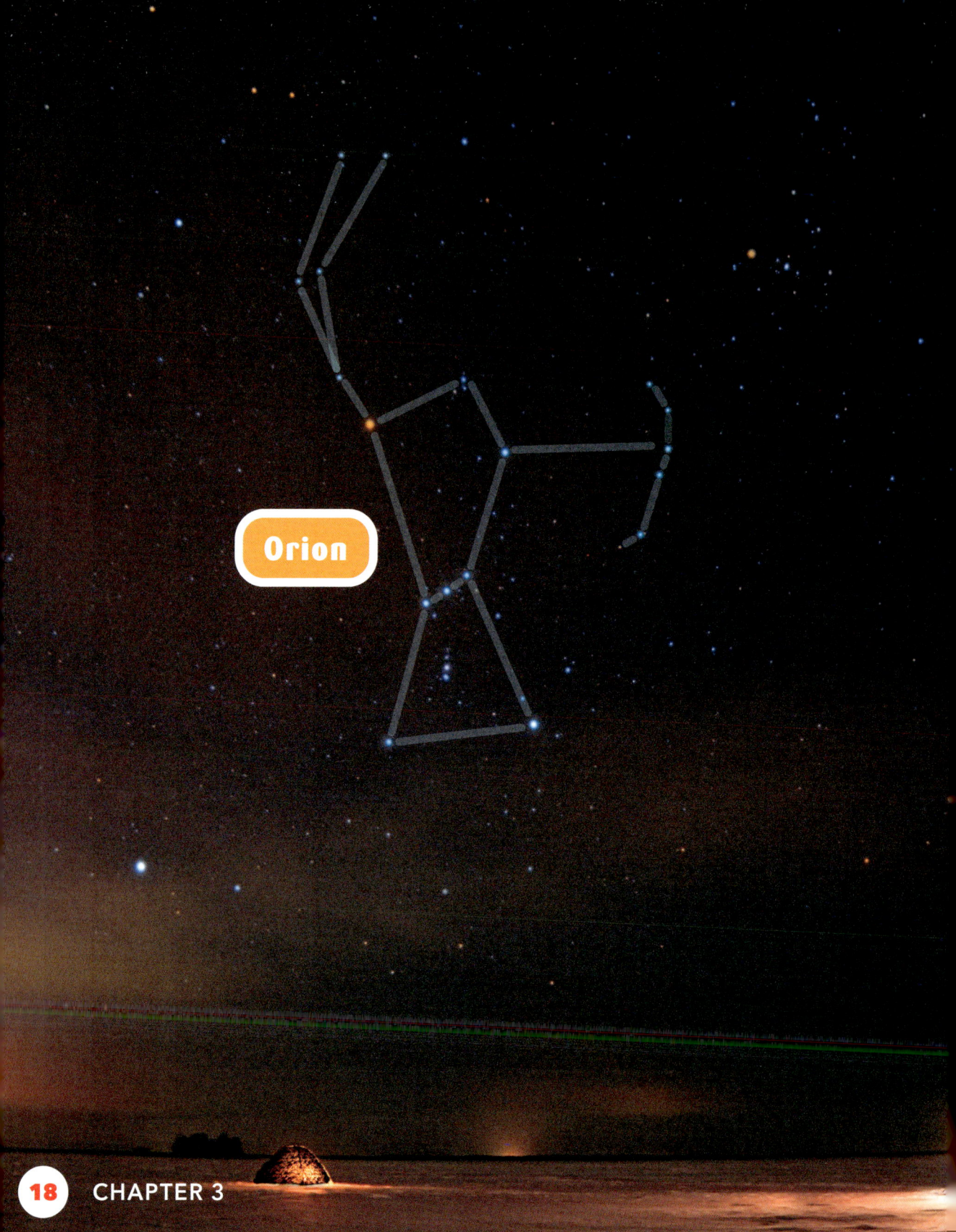

Other constellations are **seasonal**. They move in the sky over the course of a year. Orion is one. We can clearly see it in winter. Orion looks like a hunter. Do you see the bow and arrow?

> **DID YOU KNOW?**
>
> Ancient farmers used seasonal constellations. How? Their appearance let farmers know when to plant and harvest crops.

CHAPTER 3

TAKE A LOOK!

Not sure where to find constellations? Use a star map!

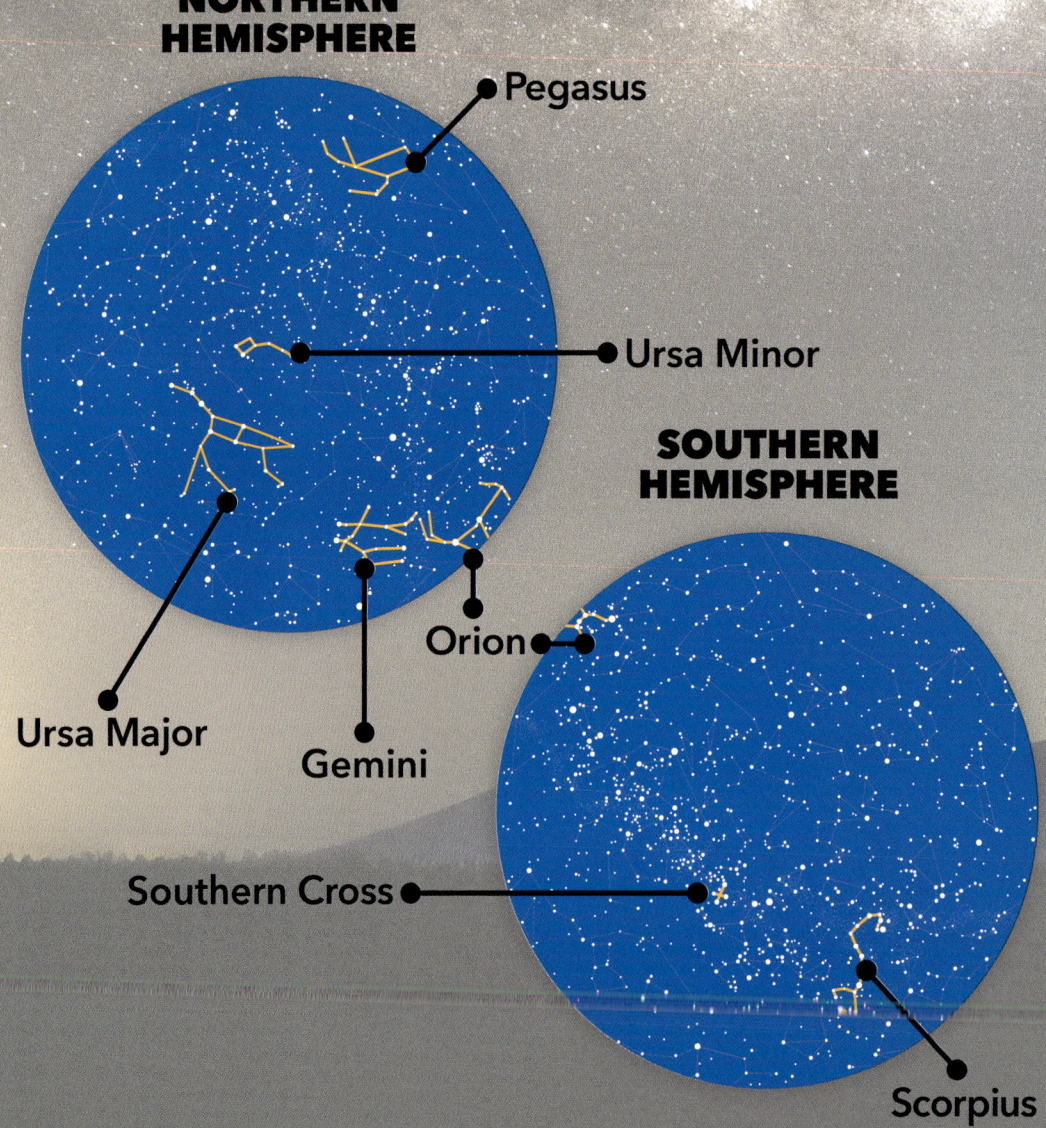

CHAPTER 3

Stars have been in approximately the same locations for thousands of years. Look up. When you see the constellations, you see what ancient people saw. Can you find a constellation?

ACTIVITIES & TOOLS

TRY THIS!

WHICH IS BRIGHTER?

A star's magnitude depends on how far it is from Earth and how much energy it has. See how this works with flashlights!

What You Need:
- a dark room
- four flashlights (two big and two small)
- a friend

1. Darken a room. Hold one of the bigger flashlights. Have your friend hold the other.

2. Stand close to a wall, shining the flashlights on the wall.

3. Have your friend take five steps back. Which light appears brighter?

4. Shine one of the smaller flashlights on the wall while your friend stays in place. Which light appears brighter?

5. Work through various situations with different distances and flashlights to see how magnitude and luminosity affect how the light appears on the wall. What do you notice?

GLOSSARY

ancient: Very old, or belonging to a period long ago.

asterism: A group of stars that forms a pattern in the sky and has a popular name but is smaller than a constellation.

astronomers: Scientists who study the stars, planets, and outer space.

constellations: Groups of visible stars that form patterns when viewed from Earth.

energy: Power from a source that produces light and heat.

luminosity: The total amount of energy that a star gives off.

magnitude: The measure of a star's brightness.

navigation: The science of determining the position of something or a distance traveled.

Northern Hemisphere: The half of Earth that is north of the equator.

point of view: A position or perspective from which something is viewed.

seasonal: Happening only in certain seasons.

Southern Hemisphere: The half of Earth that is south of the equator.

stars: Masses of burning gas visible in the sky, especially at night.

INDEX

ancient people 6, 19, 21
astronomers 6
Big Dipper 16
Earth 8, 9, 10
energy 10
Gemini 13, 20
luminosity 10
magnitude 9
navigation 16
Northern Hemisphere 16, 20
North Star 16
Orion 19, 20
Pegasus 6, 20
point of view 13
seasonal 19
Sirius 9
Southern Cross 15, 20
Southern Hemisphere 15, 20
star map 20
stars 4, 5, 8, 9, 10, 13, 16, 20, 21
stories 6
sun 8
Ursa Major 16, 20
Ursa Minor 16, 20

TO LEARN MORE

Finding more information is as easy as 1, 2, 3.
1. Go to www.factsurfer.com
2. Enter "constellations" into the search box.
3. Click the "Surf" button to see a list of websites.

ACTIVITIES & TOOLS